Lisa,
Thank you
Hold on to
best is ye

Blessings!
Minister Bonnie Carr

And, Now I See

What Are You Hiding Under Your Makeup?

Bonnie Carr

Manufactured in the United States of America.

Published by
Bonnie Carr Ministries
P.O. Box 1852
Waldorf, MD 20604

ISBN: 978-0-692-75771-0

Library of Congress Control Number: 2016912173

Cover and Interior Design by Jessica Tilles/TWA Solutions.com

For additional information, preaching engagements, book orders or signing, and woman's conference speaker, contact: bonniecarrministries@gmail.com.

Dedication

I dedicate this book to...

My best friend, my ride or die, and beloved husband, Brian "Mike" Carr.

My three children: James, Mikael, and Taniya for their love, encouragement, and support of this project.

My big sister and best friend, Michele Williams for always being there to talk to me and make me feel better, and has stepped into the role of our mother.

My father, Ralph Smith, whom God has continued to bless and we are truly grateful for the example of what a true father should be.

The memory of my loving mother, Virginia L. Smith, my big brother, the "gentle giant" Reginald (Reggie) Smith, my namesake and cousin, Dr. Bonita B. Franks, who always told me I was beautiful even when I didn't believe it. Also, her sister, Dr. Ruth Franks, who always encouraged me to continue my education and pursue all of my goals.

To all the women hiding behind their makeup, but who are willing and determined not to let the makeup define who God has created them to be.

Acknowledgments

The Lord has placed many people in my path who have played an instrumental role in my life (you know who you are). While on this journey, they have poured into my life in a mighty way. Their prayers and support over the years has inspired and motivated me to complete this beginning phase of my new ministry.

I respect and love each of you. Thank you, and may the Lord continue to bless you in a mighty way. However, I would be remiss if I did not highlight the following people: My spiritual father in ministry, Pastor Rev. Dr. Lee P. Washington of Reid Temple AME Church, Glenn Dale, Maryland, my father in ministry, Pastor Antione Hutchins of Christian Unity Baptist Church, Waldorf, Maryland, cousin Apostle Dr. Caretha Crawford, cousin Apostle Benson Kornegay, Pastor Aaron Jones, friend and mentor Rev. Avonda Thompson, cousin Lena Barros, Lorice Parker, Patricia Saunders, and, last but not least, my bestie/sister whom has encouraged, prayed, cried and pushed me to write this book through hiding behind my makeup, Jackie Jamison.

Contents

Introduction 13

Chapter 1: My Story! The Early Years 15

Chapter 2: Non-conception 20

Chapter 3: Adoption 25

Chapter 4: The Journey Through the Loss of My Mother 29

Chapter 5:Hiding Behind the Makeup 37

Chapter 6: It's a Cover Up...From a Cosmetic Spiritual Point of View 42

Chapter 7: And, Now I See...Putting on Makeup God's Way (God's Makeover) 47

Self-Assessment 51

And, Now I See

What Are You Hiding Under Your Makeup?

Bonnie Carr

"Trust in the Lord with all thine heart; and lean not unto thine own understanding.
[6]In all thy ways acknowledge him, and he shall direct thy paths."

– Proverbs 3:5-6

INTRODUCTION

This project was birthed out of my passion toward women of all ages, ethnicity, and backgrounds who are hiding behind their makeup. The Lord has given me a supernatural "makeover" and instructed me to share this vision and my testimony. This transformation did not occur over night. There were many days of praying, crying, fasting, and meditating on God's Word before the vision of beginning my new ministry to encourage, support, and empower women all over the country was revealed.

I am sharing my testimony of how God delivered me from masking my pain under my makeup. Women today mask their pains with makeup very well and, deep down inside, they are broken and holding on to bondage. This tool is to let you know you are not alone in this journey we call life. You do not have to stay broken and stuck being angry about your past.

You do not have to walk around with your head down and masking your emotions of being raped, drug addiction, divorce, broken relationships, isolating yourself from people, which leads to depression, low self-esteem, suicidal thoughts, sexual identity, visions of having an abortion, prostitution, child molestation, being child barren, and forgiveness. This is just a few. There are many other emotions we are wearing under our makeup.

Some women are still walking around with anger and rage in their hearts. You cannot move on into another relationship until you deal and heal from your past hurts. I understand anger is a natural emotion, but it is not healthy, mentally and physically. Did you know chronic anger, which is prolonged, can impact the immune system and cause other mental disorders? Please remember, when you're angry you are in control, but when you're in rage, it controls you.

I had to realize I had to take off the mask that was hindering me from my destiny. I no longer wanted to look into the wrong mirror while applying my makeup in hiding my hurts and pain. I chose to forgive myself and have a deeper relationship with God. This was the start of my healing and deliverance. Now, when I look into the mirror, I love whom I see. The enemy wanted me to stay in a state of depression, low self-esteem, hurt, anger, and etc. However, the Lord wanted me to see whom He has created and predestined me to be.

CHAPTER 1

My Story!
The Early Years

I was born and raised in Waterbury, Connecticut. I am the youngest of five siblings and, thank God, I was raised in a two-parent home. My mother was stern and when she spoke, she meant what she said. I thought she was the meanest person in the world until I grew older. I realize she wanted the best for my siblings and me. My dad has a quiet spirit, but when he spoke, everyone listened. In my childhood, the belt was used without hesitation; my mother and father believed in God and our spiritual foundation is what my family was built on.

A God fearing woman, my mother taught us about God and the power in prayer. She told my siblings and me to read the Bible because it had everything in there we needed to know and it would give us strength when we were going through tough times. We attended church mostly every Sunday. My parents made us go. My mother was on the Senior Usher Board and she took my sister and me, or just me, to other churches when there was an usher anniversary. I really didn't feel like going, but I had no choice. Now that I'm older, I realize she was planting that seed and preparing me for ministry. I always knew I had a calling on my life, but it was not until I accepted my prophetic calling from the Lord in May 2013 that I decided to stop running from it.

Growing up, I was average height and petite; I could never gain weight. My family members were bigger than me, and I always asked my mother why I was so petite. She told me when she was growing up she was tall and thin so that's why I am developed this way. I got upset when kids teased me about my size and my mother always encouraged me and explained that she was teased as well. She was called "Olive Oil" because she was tall and thin, but she didn't let it bother her. She gained weight after giving birth to five children. People of all ages, sizes, ethnic backgrounds, religious beliefs, etc., are teased or bullied every day. Bullying can have a devastating impact on people. I feel as though adults are the biggest culprits of bullying. While in middle school, a group of girls always called me skinny Minnie, bony girl, and a stuck up "B." They also called me ugly and said I had big poopy eyes. One of the girls asked me if I ate because I was so thin. This was very annoying and frustrating to have to go to school and hear these harmful comments every day. Those girls were a bunch of bullies.

I will never forget when some of the girls would walk by me and brush against me to start a fight. This one particular girl did this and she didn't think I would push her back, but my mother told me if anyone hits me, to hit them back and defend myself. One thing led to another and we wound up fighting. Students were yelling: *fight, fight.* I won the fight and I didn't get suspended, but the girl did because she started it. Also, my parents made the principal aware of the teasing from these girls. It's funny how after the fight, the girl wanted to be friends with me. Really? Now you want to be my friend.

I thought the name-calling would stop in high school, but no, other girls called me "white girl" because of my complexion and the middle-class neighborhood where I lived. I was the only African American on the cheerleading squad, at one point, and they really called me "white girl" and accused me of thinking I was better than my peers. Some of the boys also made derogatory statements toward me, such as, "you're so skinny," and "you don't have a sexy shape."

I was so sick of the verbal abuse, they call bullying, from some of my classmates. I always felt misunderstood because the girls who teased me thought I was conceited and I thought I was better than them. My classmates failed to realize words hurt a person's self-esteem and could cause a damage that's hard to heal or irreversible. I began to feel like I didn't fit in or wasn't pretty enough.

Even now as an adult, people still have something to say about my weight, and the painful affects still linger. I don't think it would be nice if I said, "Well, look how fat you are, you need to go on a diet." Despite that being a large portion of my growing up years, I had a great childhood. I took dancing lessons, was a cheerleader in high school, graduated from college with an Associate's Degree, and worked at a dental office. I was also the cheerleading coach of my former high school for three years. The young ladies trusted me and sought advice from me. The girls I mentored were very bonded to me and in some instances felt more comfortable sharing information with me than their own parents. I should have known then God was preparing me for ministry.

I relocated from Connecticut to Maryland the summer of 1992. I lived with my Aunt Daisy who also helped me get a government job. Yes, I had a government job. I worked as a Social Service Assistant for an agency. While there were times I got homesick, I did make new friends, learned new experiences, and, best of all, I met my husband, Brian Michael

Carr. He is the man who swept me off my feet. We have been married for twenty-three years, we have three adopted children (I will discuss that later), and reside in Southern Maryland.

I finally accepted the call from God in May 2013. I am a minister and doing the work God has called me to do. On December 9, 2015, I graduated from Newburgh Theological Seminary and Bible College with a Bachelor's of Arts Degree in Christian Counseling.

Chapter 2

Non-Conception

My husband, Mike, and I were married for about three years or more when we started trying to start a family. After many years of trying to get pregnant, we could never conceive. We prayed every month I would be pregnant, but God didn't answer our prayers. My gynecologist suggested we make an appointment with an infertility specialist. Mike had his sperm tested and, as the nurse told him from the results, his "soldiers were marching." Nothing was wrong with his sperm count. I had several tests done. One test result showed I had a small fibroid and polyps around my uterus, of which the doctor wanted to perform surgery. I was nervous and scared, but I prayed to God and told Him I didn't want to have surgery.

Philippians 4:6 says, *"Do not be anxious about anything, but in every situation, by prayer and petition, with thanksgiving, present your request to God."* I am so thankful and grateful I accepted Jesus Christ as my Savoir at a young age. I have a relationship with Him and I can talk with Him about anything. I trust and believe He will answer if it's His will and I believe the Word of God.

My Testimony from Test Results

The infertility doctor wanted me to take one more test before they scheduled the surgery. Two weeks passed and I was nervous and staying prayerful. One particular Sunday, I attended church service, as usual, and at the end of the Pastor's sermon, he asked everyone to lay hands on the area needing healing. I laid my hand on my stomach and, as the Pastor was praying, God spoke to me in my ear and said, "You are healed!" I trusted and believed I was healed. I held on to my faith.

Finally, I went back to the scheduled doctor's appointment, and while the doctor was performing the procedure, he looked at my husband and me and said, "I don't see anything." I could have jumped off that examination table. The fibroid tumor and the polyps around my uterus were gone. My husband and I couldn't get out of the office quick enough to give God praise.

There may be someone reading this book who doesn't believe in God. I pray this book serves as a tool to help lead you to Christ. I suggest you accept Jesus Christ as your Savoir Isaiah 53:5 says, "*But he* was *wounded for our transgressions*, he was *bruised for our iniquities: the chastisement of our peace* was *upon him; and with his stripes we are healed.*"

My husband and I were so thankful and grateful that I was healed. We kept trying after that and I still didn't get pregnant. The specialist suggested we try invitro or artificial insemination. I declined and wanted to keep the faith and trusting and believing that God would open my womb. This caused more stress on my body, as well as on my marriage.

At some point in time, I became angry with God because He showed me that I would have a child and it didn't come to pass. I found myself being stressed, bitter, and angry with my husband. I would get upset when I would hear the news of a family member or friends who became pregnant and I wasn't. I was happy to hear and upset at the same time, if that makes any sense. I am sure you have been there where God never answered your prayers or you're still waiting. I even shut down from my husband. Some days I would find myself depressed about the situation. I asked God, *Why me? How come I couldn't conceive and have the experience of giving birth to a child?* I would just walk around with a smile on my face, hiding behind my makeup like I wasn't hurting from this pain. Sometimes going to baby showers would bother me. I even gave my sister her baby shower. I will never forget that someone had asked me how I felt that my sister was pregnant and she had gotten married after me and starting a family before me. I answered with a smile and said, "She is older than me and wanted to start a family right away." People are not sensitive to questions they ask. They didn't know if I had several miscarriages or if I had a baby that was still born. I may have had a hysterectomy and can't have any children.

I really had to ask God to help me out of this funk. I thank God for restoring me over time and now I am seeing things differently. Once I sincerely reached a point in my life of understanding that God loves me and saw the real me beneath my mask of makeup, I was able to freely take it off. I was able to receive His true makeover.

I had to grow to a point and realize that God's timing is not our timing. God has a reason for everything in our lives. We may not understand why we go through pain and hurt in our lives. God showed me in the process that I have a very supportive and loving husband. My husband, Mike, would always encourage me, and work hard to keeping a positive attitude so he wouldn't get down on himself. I thank God for a saved husband who loves me in spite of my mess and what I'm going through and being able to love me through my makeup. I didn't realize he felt badly also, but he didn't show it like I did.

I was so into my own feelings and pity party that I didn't think to ask my husband how he felt about the situation.

I felt less of a woman because I didn't give birth to a child. But, after God spoke to me and by talking to other women who also desired to have children, I didn't feel alone. There are people going through the same pain I went through. It may not have been child bearing. It could simply be holding on to a not yet fulfilled promise. Meaning that the thing (situation) you prayed about has not been answered yet, but you are keeping the faith that the blessing is going to come to pass. Know that you are not alone.

Chapter 3

Adoption

"He predestined us to be adopted as his sons through Jesus Christ, in accordance with his pleasure and will." – Ephesians 1:5

The Lord spoke through a minister and friend at the church we attended at that time. She approached us and said that God told her to mention to us about possibly adopting. After praying for guidance, my husband and I moved forward in the pursuit of adoption. Throughout the process, the Lord gave us confirmation about our decision. I say this because you hear all kinds of stories about how stressful the process of adoption can be, but it moved quickly and painless for us.

I remember the mounting feelings of anxiety and excitement at the beginning of the adoption process. Once

Mike and I started participating in the pre-service training classes, those feelings slowly started to subside. I think it was a combination of familiar information which lead to good discussions in class. The other key for me was that I was able to use my organizational skills to keep up with and complete all the required documentations. Not to mention Mike knew some of the staff instructors in the program. The time seemed to pass by quicker than we anticipated. Overall, our experience with the licensing process was fairly enjoyable.

God gave us double for our trouble. We planned to adopt one boy, but then the agency informed us that the boy we were adopting had a sibling that would be born soon. The agency asked if we wanted to adopt the sibling as well. Mike and I discussed it and by him being a social worker, he said it was best to keep the siblings together. So, we adopted two-year-old James and his infant brother, Mikael. It was like having twins. James was still in pampers and I had to potty train him. After being placed in several foster homes, he had witnessed something traumatic that gave him night terrors. Mikael was placed with us and he had several medical issues, so I constantly had to bring him to the doctors. It was not easy going from no children to two with special needs. Mike and I questioned ourselves. Should we have done this? But God brought us through with the laying of hands on these children with prayer and especially love. We always speak life into our children. Once we finalized the adoption, we realized from a spiritual standpoint, that the Lord loves us and adopted us. Our two sons really have testimonies. The enemy really tried to take them out, but God chose us to love and raise them as the men they will be with God in their lives.

When the boys were placed in our home, I chose to be a stay-at-home mom to bond with them and attend to their needs. I will never forget my last day of work. The Lord spoke to me and said, "You will never want for nothing." I'm here to tell you God has truly blessed us since the boys have become part of our family. The Lord has continued to bless us with supplying all our financial needs. As my boys grew older and went to school full time, I decided to seek a part-time job to get out of the house. I started getting lazy and I was doing the same routine. I started losing my sense of self, even shopping got boring at times. I can honestly say that being a stay-at-home mom is not an easy job. I started working part time for two years and the boys loved that I would bring them to school and pick them up. I also decided to go back to college. I was working and taking a few college classes.

It's funny how the Lord has a sense of humor. My two sons, who were eight and six years old at the time, kept telling us they wanted a sister. We looked at them like they were crazy. The boys alone were enough to take care of. They were independent and I didn't have to worry about pampers, formula, potty training, etc. Those infant and toddler days were over, or so we thought. I received a phone call from a family member to see if Mike and I could adopt his daughter. What? Really? So we went back on our journey of praying and asking God for guidance in this situation. This baby had some medical issues at birth. She was born premature, and she would require a lot of care. God spared her life and had already prepared us to be parents. Our sons received their sister and, once again, God made us parents.

CHAPTER 4

The Journey Through the Loss of My Mother

When I received the call from Michele, my sister, telling me that our mother, Virginia, had taken ill and she had to be taken by ambulance to the hospital, I felt so hopeless I couldn't get to the hospital because I lived six hours away, in a different state. I was actually on my way to a Christmas event with Mike and our sons, and we had stopped at the gas station when I received the call. The event was about an hour away. My anxiety rose because we didn't know what was wrong with her. I could count on my fingers how many times Mom had to go to the hospital. She was diagnosed with Alzheimer's disease so she couldn't tell my dad or my brother when she wasn't feeling well. That particular day, she was non-responsive. I told

Mike I didn't want to go to the party, I just didn't feel right, and I wanted to be at home. I felt bad; I live in Maryland and my parents and siblings live in Connecticut. When this happened, I wanted to be there with "my ride or die," my best friend, my mom.

A couple hours later, Michele called me back to let me know of Mom's progress after having many tests done. She didn't call with good news. She informed me one of Mom's lungs had collapsed and she was on a ventilator to help her breathe, and she could pass away that night or the next day. Mom had a pulmonary embolism, which was a blood clot that had traveled to her left lung. I cried in disbelief that this was actually happening. I really thought this was a dream. Michele asked if there was any way I could get a flight to Connecticut to see Mom before she goes home to be with the Lord. I told her I would get back to her. I hung up the phone and explained to Mike what was going on with Mom's progress and he hugged me and told me he was so sorry to hear this because he knew how close my mother and I were. I talked to her about anything and she gave me great advice about life.

I had to call my friends to let them know what was going on. They were praying for me and wanted me to keep them posted on her progress. My friend, Avonda, stopped what she was doing and came to visit. She prayed with me and she also was trying to look up flights for me to get to Connecticut, but

God had me just sitting on my bed, being still. Avonda asked if I felt at peace with not seeing my mother for the last time. I said yes because I believe God didn't want me to see her hooked up to the ventilator.

I patiently waited for an update on Mom, I will never forget the call back from Michele, stating Mom's pressure was dropping and she was slipping away, and my dad had to make the decision to take her off the ventilator to let her pass.

"If he is at peace with it, and I can't get there in time, then go ahead and let her rest with the Lord," I said to Michele.

While on the phone with Michele, they had started the process of taking Mom off the ventilator.

"Mom has passed peacefully," Michele said.

"Okay," I said and hung up the phone.

I cried and cried, because I couldn't believe this had happened. My lifeline had left me. I felt so lost and alone; I wanted to hear her voice just one more time. The thought of that not happening again devastated beyond anything I could imagine.

I began to think about my childhood days with Mom. I am the baby of my siblings and I was always attached to her hip. Even when she lay down on the couch, I always lay down next to her. As I grew older into my teenage years, she always brought Michele and me grocery and clothes shopping. People would call us the Three Musketeers. We were always together doing something. Mom also taught me how to cook, bake, and be self-sufficient.

When I was on my high school cheerleading team for basketball and football seasons, Mom was always there to cheer me on. I felt so special and loved that she would show up and support me, especially when she would sit outside in the freezing cold during football season to watch me cheer. She would cheer with us while drinking her hot chocolate.

I thank God that I could talk to my mom about anything I was going through, especially dealing with dating or if I had a crush on someone. She gave me great advice about boys during my adolescent years. She didn't bite her tongue. She would tell you like it is pertaining to boys and men in general. During my adult years, she told me: "When you pray and ask God to send you a man to marry in your life, be specific because you don't want God to send you just any ol' man." I will never forget that conversation.

My siblings would tease me about being spoiled by our mother. Why not? I was her baby girl! They used to call me "little Virginia." Mom protected me, fought for me when people would do me wrong, provided for me and, most of all, she loved me unconditionally. Once, when I came home from school, feeling sad from being teased about my weight, she spoke life of encouraging words to make me feel better about myself. She said, "Never worry about what people say about you." She always reminded me of how beautiful and special I was to her and in God's eyes. I truly miss our talks, going to the hair and nail salons, traveling, and even our little disagreements, which led her to hanging up on me sometimes. I still laugh about how she would hang up on me.

I have to admit, after the loss of Mom, I walked around pretending to be okay. In reality, I was simply hiding behind my makeup with being frustrated, angry, hurt and lost. I felt like my heart was being ripped apart, piece by piece. I was really wearing my mask of makeup hiding my feelings of depression and loneliness.

I remember my first Mother's Day without my mother, which was five months after her passing. I started feeling anxious about the month of May approaching. I said, "I wish the month of May would hurry up and go by fast." My friends were talking about what their plans were and asking each other what gifts they were buying for their mother. "Hello! I'm standing right here. Umm, remember me? My mother has passed away!!??!" I know I shouldn't expect everyone to stop talking about their mother because of the loss of my mother, and I can't expect these things aren't going to come up in a conversation. But still, it hurts. I would feel saddened when I would see Mother's Day commercials on television. When I would go to the store, I would try to avoid walking by the beautiful stationary of Mother's Day cards and the beautiful flowers. I always sent Mom flowers and a card if I couldn't make the trip to see her. Mom always told my siblings and me to give her flowers while she was living because once she was no longer with us, she would not be able to smell them.

I also would get emotional when I would see a mother and daughter together, having a great time. I was getting a pedicure and a woman walked in with her elder mother and told the owner they were both getting a pedicure and she was treating her mother to a pedicure and manicure for Mother's Day. I had to hold back my tears. I said, "Why, Lord, did this have to happen to me? If I could just talk and see my mother one more time." Mom and I used to go to the nail salon, so this brought back great memories. I decided to do this as a custom and reflect on the good times we shared together. Even though I am a mother of three beautiful children, I had to fight the pain of my heart being shattered into pieces. I wore my makeup well with the struggle of Mom's death.

Life has a way of unexpected things to happen in our lives. Maybe you haven't experienced a loss of a mother, but you have experienced a loss of a father, spouse, grandparents, aunt, uncle, nephew, brother, sister, and even a loss of your child. Some of you may have experienced the loss of your job due to layoffs. We don't understand life's unexpected events. However, God can comfort us in the midst of these losses.

I had to press through my pain of hiding under my makeup of my broken heart. It has not been easy, but God has been my healer, deliverer, and comforter. Without Him, I thought I was going to lose my mind. I had to get to a point of my faith walk with the Lord to trust Him and believe He will heal my broken heart that had been torn apart into pieces. It is fine to cry and be sad. This doesn't mean I am weak. It means I am getting stronger and I can overcome this just like anything else.

God told me to stay focused, trust and worship Him through my pain and everything else will follow. As the years has gone by from the loss of Mom, it has been a little easier, not that I don't miss her because sometimes I still can't believe she is gone and I still see images of her in the casket. I'm still in disbelief. But, in reality, it is true and we all have a death date. I know I have a resting place in heaven and I do believe I will see her and my loved ones again. This is where I feel the joy in my heart.

God said He would be a comforter and He sure was and He still is. I miss Mom so much, but as I grew closer with having a relationship with God, I thanked Him for giving me a precious gift for a season of forty years of my life. I will never forget the date of Mom death date: December 16, 2006.

If your mother and father are still living, cherish every moment with them. But, there's something about the loss of your mother. The one whom gave birth or even adopted mother whom loved you unconditionally. If you don't have a close relationship with your mother, please ask God to let go of whatever you're holding onto in your heart. Someone may have a situation where you weren't raised by your biological mother, but for whatever reason you were raised by your grandparents, a relative, foster care. Now fathers are raising their children as well. You may be hiding bitterness, anger, and frustration under your makeup. Please forgive your mother or ask her to forgive you for your actions toward her.

You see, once your mother closes her eyes and leaves this side of Zion that is it. No more talks, laughs, spending quality time together, or phone calls. Under your makeup, you will carry around the pain of guilt, regrets, and would've-could've-should've. If you look at it from a spiritual point of view, Exodus 20:12 says, *"Honor your father and your mother, so you may live long in the land the Lord your God is giving you."* Please get your relationship right with your mother so you can be at peace if something were to happen to her.

CHAPTER 5

Hiding Behind the Makeup

As women, we walk around smiling like nothing is wrong with us. One minute we are laughing, joking, happy, and the next thing you know, we are angry, sad, disappointed, and disgusted. The truth be told, we are spiritually bipolar. We are up and then we are down and depressed, hiding behind our makeup. You ask that sister how is she doing, and she tells you. "I'm fine." She is F.I.N.E all right. She is Frustrated, Irritated, Neurotic, and Exhausted. We need to be true with ourselves; we are all jacked up. As women, we wear our makeup well, hiding under the layers of foundation, blush, eye shadow, eyeliner, mascara, false eyelashes, and lipstick. Deep down inside we are still carrying around our hurts and pain from our past.

Some of you reading this book may have experiences as a single parent, may have lost a loved one, been a victim of child abuse, experienced anxiety, have mental health issues, experienced sexual abuse, been involved with drugs, have low self-esteem, dealing with broken relationships, identify sexuality, going through depression, domestic violence, oppression, miscarriages, and divorce. You may have even experienced an abortion, your spouse walked out on you, you were date raped, or you cheated on your spouse or your spouse cheated on you. Some of us carrying that shame and guilt around every day. You may have shared with a friend or sought professional counseling, but until you learn to see yourself in the manner in which the Lord sees you, the pain will continue to manifest itself.

I have spoken a lot about makeup. I have alluded to cover-up and all of the things that makeup does. It provides the illusion of beauty and perfection. It hides the imperfection and makes others feel good. As I talked about makeup in my story, it did something else for me. It allowed me to hide my shame, my disappointment, my fears, and insecurities. It kept me from dealing with my inner pain. Now, I am in a different place, a better place and it is time we take off the makeup and unmask.

Well, ladies, it's time to remove the layers of makeup and give those layers of bondage over to God and let Him give you a holy makeover. Until we deal with those hurts and pains, and seek God for deliverance, we are going to keep wearing our makeup to try to cover up our flaws. We hide them from the world, but God knows our flaws. Jesus died on the cross for every sin we have committed in our lives. Thank you, Jesus, for dying on the cross because He knew we would sin, and just know we are not going to stay in bondage. John 8:36 says, *"Therefore if the Son sets you free, you will be free indeed."* Let go and let God heal, deliver, and set you free of those hurts and pains in which we call bondage. We are dealing with spiritual warfare. We tell God to deliver us from our hurt and pain, but the enemy continues to fill our heads with negativity. Telling us we're ugly, we're not good enough, we're never going to make it, we're too skinny, we're too fat, we're going to die, we're really not healed from our past, we can't pursue that new career move, we will never get off drugs, and so on. I'm not ashamed to admit I was once held captive by negative thoughts until I came to realize who I was in the Lord. The example that comes to mind is in Luke 15:16-17 about the Prodigal Son. Pigs spend a lot of time making squealing sounds and eating. Their diet includes all types of unhealthy things. In other words, they enjoy or are comfortable with consuming garbage. In this scripture passage, the Lord shares the parable to His disciples about the Prodigal Son in how this man made poor choices and because of his guilt found himself one day eating with the swine. Once he realized who his Father was, he immediately left the "pig feast" and sought after Him. This story is so prevalent in our daily lives. We continually hang out with people who mean us no good, or "act out" in destructive ways. The only way this pattern can change is when we, like that Prodigal Son, learn to see ourselves the way our Heavenly Father sees us.

In the story of the Prodigal Son, the youngest man's father prayed for his son's return. Because of his unconditional love for him, he gave his son a welcoming home party. In summary of this story is that Jesus loves us and wants us to trust Him by taking off our masks. The Lord's desire is for us to discover who we are in Him. (*"I am fearfully and wonderfully made,"* Psalms 139:14.) Therefore, knowing we no longer have to dine with pigs. The Lord wants us to be overcomers. 1 John 5:4, *"For everyone born of God overcomes the world."* This is the victory that has overcome the world, even our faith.

My Testimony

I once suffered with anxiety attacks, low self-esteem, thinking about my past hurts from a relationship, or even how family members have treated me. I remember when I thought I was going to die from what I thought was a heart attack, but it was an anxiety attack. I had tingling in my arms, neck, shoulders, chest pain, shortness of breath, all due to stress. I believed this was the trick of the enemy trying to take me out, but sometimes it's not always the enemy. God will allow adversaries to come into your life to test your faith and to see if you are going to depend on Him to help you and set you free from bondage. God placed encouraging people in my life to speak life and study the Word of God. Once I began to take on this habit, my anxiety began to lessen. I wouldn't get upset about every little thing. I wasn't letting disappointment get me depressed nor was I having pity parties because I couldn't have my way. I had to learn how to trust, believe, and depend on God for everything in my life, in spite of the situation.

You may not believe in God, may be angry with God, may have backslidden, or stopped going to church. I suggest you try Him for yourself. Try Him again and in a different way. Experience a new and better relationship with Him. What do you have to lose? A relationship with God will cost not nearly as much as spending money to hide behind the makeup.

After reading my story of my hiding behind the makeup, I pray you are now ready to have a makeover God's way. Will you give those flaws that have you bound, hidden, and covered up under your mask of makeup to Him? If you say you don't wear makeup, did you know the smile you hide behind does the same thing as foundation, blush or lipstick? It hides and conceal what is truly there. The Lord's makeover is a healing of both physical and spiritual transformation.

Chapter 6

It's a Cover Up... From a Cosmetic Spiritual Point of View

From a cosmetic point of view, makeup can be like magic. It can make you look like a completely different person, depending on how much you use. Some women like to apply layers and layers of makeup to hide who they really are, which means they are usually not happy with themselves. Makeup can be used to beautify. Some woman use makeup to lighten their skin because they think they are too dark. Makeup is a cover-up. The good news is Jesus looks beyond your faults, and what you think are your flaws. Jesus is always by your side and loves you through your pain.

Here is a list of how makeup is defined from a cosmetic point of view to cover up your flaws and how you can apply your makeup from a spiritual point of view when you start to see things differently when God gives you a holy makeover.

Foundation: is a skin-colored cosmetic applied to the face to create an even, uniform color to the complexion to cover flaws and sometimes to change the natural skin tone. Applying your foundation from a spiritual point of view with God's makeover, you have to come to realize who created the foundation, which is Jesus Christ. 1 Corinthians 3:11 (NIV) says, *"For no one can lay any foundation other than the one already laid, which is Jesus Christ."* When you see your foundation of your life is starting to crack, and you have established Jesus Christ is your foundation, know Jesus can mend those cracks in your life with the holy foundation. You have the power to place the foundation on your face once you establish whom your foundation is. Now you can start applying your foundation with confidence because now you know God loves you just the way He created you, and you are set free of those bondage. So, my sister, apply the foundation by saying, *"I am fearfully and wonderfully made,"* (Psalm 139:14).

***Eyeliner*:** is a cosmetic used to define the eyes. It is applied around the contours of the eye(s) to create a variety of aesthetic effects. The makeup is usually used by women and girls. It comes in different colors. When you're applying your eyeliner from the spiritual, God will line you up with the right people and connect you with a church to fellowship with God and other people. God will separate you from those negative people and line you up with positive people to help you with your low self-esteem or whatever you're going through. You don't need to associate with negative people whom can bring your spirit down because eventually you will start being negative and toxic. You heard of "misery loves company." It's not that you're better than anyone else, you need to stay focus on your deliverance because the enemy will try and bring you back down lower than you ought to be. You need to speak life into your situation. When you wake up in the morning, the first thing you should do is thank and seek God first in your life to fill your thoughts with His desires. Once you start lining yourself with God, you can apply your eyeliner with determination by saying, *"But seek first the kingdom of God and his righteousness, and all these things shall be added to you"* (Matthew 6:33).

***Eye Shadow*:** is a cosmetic that is applied on the eyelids and under the eyebrows. It is commonly used to make the wearers eyes stand out or look more attractive. Eye shadow can add depth and dimension to one's eyes, complement the eye color or simply draw attention to the eyes. It comes in different colors and textures and it can be found in liquid, pencil, or mousse form. When applying the eye shadow from the spiritual, you can place your eye shadow once God opens your eyes to see that you are beautiful. You can see that you can be delivered from drug addiction, adultery, and prostitution. God will let you see that you don't have to live like that anymore. God can heal you from your past of what you see when you look in the mirror every day. God will allow you to open your eyes to see the goodness in you. You no longer have to walk around with your head hung low. Lift your head up and see greatness in yourself. Eye shadow comes in three shades: the Father, the Son, and the Holy Ghost. Now you can apply your eye shadow with certainty by saying, *"I once was lost, but now am found. Was blind but now I see,"* (John 9:25).

Blush/Rouge/Blusher: is a cosmetic typically used by women to redden the cheeks to provide a more youthful appearance, and to emphasize the cheekbones. Blush highlights the cheekbones. When applying blush from the spiritual, remember God has brought out the best in you. God knows the plans that He has for your life to be *"the head and not the tail"* (Deuteronomy 28:13). Stop holding on to your past situation. God has broken the chains that had you bound. The chains of your past of broken relationship, depression, lows self-esteem, and drug addiction have fallen off your cheeks. Once you let go and let God settle the score, you can stop rehearsing your past. Now you can apply your blush with assurance that

"Old things have passed away, behold all things are become new" (2 Corinthians 5:17)

Lipstick: is a cosmetic product containing pigments, oils, waxes, and emollients that apply color, texture, and protection to the lips. Many colors and types of lipstick exist. It is worn by women. When applying your lipstick from the spiritual, your lips are part of your mouth. Your mouth should be used to speak life to yourself and others. Speak positive thoughts such as, "I am beautiful, I will be successful, I will get that new job, I can go back to school, and I am healed from my infirmities." You can speak to that nasty devil and say, "You will no longer have power over me." Tell that devil you will no longer have anxiety attacks, no more depression, no more drug abuse, no more living in fear, and no more prostitution. You will no longer live in bondage; the chains are broken and you are set free. No more holding onto baggage, weighing you down. Open up your suitcase full of bondage, unpack them, throw them out, and give them to God. Tell the devil that you have unpacked your suitcase with all those heavy burdens that were holding you down and because God lives, you can face tomorrow. God holds the future and you have the victory. You shall live and not die. Now you can apply your lipstick with the authority by saying, *"I can do all things through Christ that strengthens me"* (Philippians 4:13).

Chapter 7

And, Now I See... Putting on My Makeup God's Way (God's Makeover)

Have you ever gotten to a point in your life where you just wanted to give up? You may have wanted to give up on your marriage, your children, your job, your ministry and you may have even thought about giving up on your life. I did get to a point where I wanted to give up on a few things, such as my marriage, my children, and my ministry. I didn't like to be stressed out all the time. But, glory be to God I didn't give up. God told me I shall live and not die and He has great works for me to do for His kingdom. Be honest with yourselves, we all have been to this dark place.

As I'm growing in this Christian walk with the Lord, God had to allow things to happen in my life so He would get all the glory. I had gotten to a point to depend on God to work out my situations. I had to learn to love myself. I didn't like what I saw when I looked in the mirror. I had a complex about my size. I was hiding under my makeup; bondage that hindered me from my destiny. I had to seek God for healing and restoration. God made me and now I'm free and I love myself. Jesus loves me just the way I am. I praise God for His healing restoration and setting me free.

I bet you're reading this and saying, "Well it's not easy to get over my hurts and pains of the loss of a loved one, a broken relationship, a divorce, being raped, having low self-esteem, verbal and mentally abused, drug addiction, lying, cheating, gossiping, and the list goes on." I'm not suggesting this is going to be an easy or overnight process. However, in my case, these are the four steps I took during my transformation of God's makeover.

Step One: I had to trust God. I had to trust the process of my faith being tested. I had to trust I could be healed from my broken heart, low self-esteem, and loss of my mother, bitterness, and anger. The Bible says, "*Trust in the Lord with all your heart, lean not to your own understanding.*" I had to get to a point to trust God and lean on His Word that He would direct my path in the direction He wanted me to go and trusting He would do it.

Step Two: I had to believe. I had to trust and believe I am healed from my past relationships, anxiety, and frustration. I had to believe God is a healer, He is the Alpha and Omega, and the "I AM." Once I started believing God for who He is and what His Word says, by His stripes, I am healed. I read about the people in the Bible and one that comes to mind is the woman with the issue of blood. I said if God can dry her blood after all those years, He can do it for me! Nothing is too hard for God.

Step Three: I had to depend on God. I had to trust, believe and now depend on God. I depended on God's Word that I was fearfully and wonderfully made. I had to open my heart to depend on God. Once I started depending on God, He was showing me the manifestation and the blessings that He was giving me and opening doors with my new ministry. I had to depend on God to heal me from the loss of my mother, and from being frustrated because I could not give birth. Also being teased about my weight, which led to not feeling good about myself. I had to depend on God to let me unmask my pain and start letting Him give me a Holy makeover.

Step Four: I had to receive. I had to trust, believe, depend, and now receive all the blessings God has for me. I received Jesus Christ as my Savior at a very young age. I'm so thankful for this walk with God. I had to receive the prophetic anointing calling I have on my life. This has not been easy, but I'm now seeing and receiving all the trials and tribulations in a different way. I'm realizing this is a part of the journey, walking with God. God is still molding and shaping me to be used for His glory to minister to His people. You cannot have a testimony without being tested in your life.

Now I see I don't need to depend on a man's approval of how I look. Now I see I can move forward in the plans God has for my life. Now I see my life is not over because of the mistakes I have made in the past. Now I see with Christ I can do anything, He has already laid out my destiny. Now I see greater is He that is in me than He that is in the world. Now I see the enemy has NO power over me. Now I see God was equipping me to encourage, teach, and preach the prophetic word to His people. God wants me to speak life into the people who are hurting and hiding under their makeup. Speaking life to yourself starts your healing process. Remember, don't let the makeup wear you...you wear the makeup!

Self-Assessment

1. When you look in the mirror, what do you see? Please be honest with yourself. This is between you and God. Check off that which applies to you.

—	Bitterness	—	Depression
—	Low self-esteem	—	Disappointment
—	Guilt	—	Anger
—	Shame	—	Anxiety
—	Frustration	—	Feeling hopeless
—	Gossiper	—	Holding on to the past
—	Adulterer	—	Feelings of rejection
—	Lonely	—	Acceptance/want to "fit in"
—	Feelings of inadequacy	—	Feels you're too fat
—	In a broken relationship	—	Feels you're too skinny
—	Suicidal thoughts	—	Drug addiction

2. What are your fears/doubts?

____

____

____

____

____

____

____

____

____

3. Are you harboring negative feelings of a traumatic incident from your past?

4. Have you ever spoken death to yourself? Meaning, you're always saying negative comments about yourself.

5. Do you socialize with negative people in your circle of friends you need to let go?

____

____

____

____

____

____

____

____

____

6. Have you accepted the negative comments said about you over the years? For example, "You get it honest, you're going to be just like your mother, and she had a mean spirit."

____

____

____

____

____

____

____

____

____

7. Do you live life to please others?

8. Do you believe the Lord loves you and wants you to prosper?

9. Are you ready for God to deliver you from your bondage(s)?

10. Have you accepted Jesus Christ as your Savior? If you haven't, there is no time like the present. Romans 10:9 says, "*That if thou shalt confess with thy mouth the Lord Jesus, and shalt believe in thine heart that God hath raised him from the dead, thou shalt be saved.*"

After completing this self-assessment exercise, my prayer is that you will have a renewed desire to reconnect with the Lord. I realize each reader is at a different place of relationship with the Lord. Some of you may be on a first-name basis, where others are a distant friend. Other examples involve watching church services at home frequently or only going to church during the holiday seasons (CME's) Christmas, Mother's Day, and Easter. The Lord's desire is for you to move beyond that state of complacency. Please pray for guidance and direction of joining a local church and becoming actively involved in a ministry.

I also pray that you will start trusting, believing, depending, and receiving what God has for you. Don't give up. God has everything under control. You may not see it, but trust me, God has you. Never forget that you are a child of the Most High. Stop living in bondage. Release them over to God. Try some faith and trust in God. Rejoice in the Lord! Favor and restoration shall come upon you. It shall happen. God is faithful!

Which side do you choose? Do you choose to cover up your insecurities with makeup or let God do your makeover?

This above drawing is the original book cover concept designed by my son James Carr

67784497R00038

Made in the USA
Charleston, SC
24 February 2017